Poems of
Edgar Allan Poe

POEMS OF
EDGAR ALLAN POE

Illustrated by Edmund Dulac

GRAMERCY BOOKS
New York · Avenel

This edition is published by Gramercy Books,
distributed by Random House Value Publishing, Inc.
40 Engelhard Avenue
Avenel, New Jersey 07001

Random House
New York • Toronto • London • Sydney • Auckland

Designed by Kathryn Wolgast Plosica

Printed and bound in Singapore

Library of Congress Cataloging-in-Publication Data
Poe, Edgar Allan, 1809-1849.
[Poems. Selections]
Poems of Edgar Allan Poe.
p. cm.
Collection of 30 poems.
ISBN 0-517-12285-5
1. Fantastic poetry, American. I. Title.
PS2605.A1 1995
811'.3—dc20   94-42278
                                                    CIP

8 7 6 5 4 3 2 1

CONTENTS

INTRODUCTION

Edgar Allan Poe, the father of the detective story and the gothic tale of horror, had an affinity for verse. "With me," he wrote, "poetry has been not a purpose but a passion." Perhaps it was in poetry that he could best express his deepest emotions.

Poe's short life was marked by tragedy and misfortune. He was born in Boston on January 19, 1809, the second of three children of itinerant actors. His parents both died of tuberculosis when he was quite young and he was adopted by Frances Allan, whose husband was a prosperous tobacco merchant in Richmond, Virginia. From that point his childhood was quite comfortable and stable. He was an excellent student and his future seemed bright.

In 1826, Poe entered the University of Virginia, but his excessive drinking and quarrels with his foster father about money and his gambling debts forced him to leave after a year, whereupon he joined the army for two years. In 1830 he entered West Point, but left soon afterward because John Allan refused any financial support.

Poe's first volume of verse, *Tamerlane and Other Poems*, had been published in 1827, but it received little critical or popular notice. His literary career truly started some years later when he began to write short stories for magazines. He also worked for several major magazines

where his skills as an editor and critic gained him respect. But personal problems and poverty continued to plague him, and his alcoholism cost him several editorial jobs.

In 1836, Poe married his fourteen–year–old cousin, Virginia Clemm, but her ill health was a constant source of anxiety. Her death from tuberculosis eleven years later led to Poe's complete mental and physical breakdown. When he recovered he joined a temperance society and became engaged to his childhood sweetheart, Elmira Royston Shelton. Then, on October 3, 1849, he was found beaten unconscious in an alley and was taken to a Baltimore charity hospital, where he died four days later without ever regaining consciousness. He was forty years old.

Poe's brilliance as a poet and his enormous influence are often undermined. But, as the poet W. H. Auden wrote, "No one in his time, put so much energy and insight into making his contemporary poets take their craft seriously."

Edgar Allan Poe's poetry is rich with musical phrases. Many of his poems, including "The Raven," "The Bells," and "Annabel Lee," are among the most technically accomplished and the most popular in the English language.

In this collection, Edmund Dulac's evocative and atmospheric illustrations illuminate Poe's sensuous imagery and surreal landscapes and add a new dimension to his poems.

GAIL HARVEY

New York
1995

The Bells

I

Hear the sledges with the bells—
    Silver bells!
What a world of merriment their melody foretells!
    How they tinkle, tinkle, tinkle,
      In the icy air of night!
    While the stars, that oversprinkle
    All the heavens, seem to twinkle
      With a crystalline delight;
    Keeping time, time, time,
    In a sort of Runic rhyme,
To the tintinabulation that so musically wells
  From the bells, bells, bells, bells,
      Bells, bells, bells—
From the jingling and the tinkling of the bells.

II

Hear the mellow wedding bells,
　　Golden bells!
What a world of happiness their harmony foretells!
　　Through the balmy air of night
　　How they ring out their delight!
　　　From the molten golden-notes,
　　　　And all in tune,
　　　What a liquid ditty floats
To the turtledove that listens, while she gloats
　　　　On the moon!
　　Oh, from out the sounding cells,
What a gush of euphony voluminously wells!
　　　How it swells!
　　　How it dwells
　　On the Future! how it tells
　　Of the rapture that impels
　To the swinging and the ringing
　　Of the bells, bells, bells,
Of the bells, bells, bells, bells,
　　　Bells, bells, bells—
To the rhyming and the chiming of the bells!

III

Hear the loud alarum bells—
Brazen bells!
What a tale of terror, now, their turbulency tells!
In the startled ear of night
How they scream out their affright!
Too much horrified to speak
They can only shriek, shriek,
Out of tune,
In a clamorous appealing to the mercy of the fire,
In a mad expostulation with the deaf and frantic fire,
Leaping higher, higher, higher,
With a desperate desire,
And a resolute endeavor.
Now—now to sit or never,
By the side of the pale-faced moon.
Oh, the bells, bells, bells!
What a tale their terror tells
Of Despair!

How they clang, and clash, and roar!
What a horror they outpour
On the bosom of the palpitating air!
Yet the ear it fully knows,
By the twanging,
And the clanging,
How the danger ebbs and flows:
Yet the ear distinctly tells,
In the jangling,
And the wrangling,
How the danger sinks and swells,
By the sinking or the swelling in the anger of the bells—
Of the bells—
Of the bells, bells, bells, bells,
Bells, bells, bells—
In the clamor and the clangor of the bells!

IV

Hear the tolling of the bells—
     Iron bells!
What a world of solemn thought their monody compels!
     In the silence of the night,
     How we shiver with affright
At the melancholy menace of their tone!
     For every sound that floats
     From the rust within their throats
      Is a groan.
     And the people—ah, the people—
     They that dwell up in the steeple,
      All alone,
     And who, tolling, tolling, tolling,
      In that muffled monotone,
     Feel a glory in so rolling
      On the human heart a stone—
     They are neither man nor woman—
     They are neither brute nor human—

They are Ghouls:
And their king it is who tolls;
And he rolls, rolls, rolls,
    Rolls
            A paean from the bells!
And his merry bosom swells
    With the paean of the bells!
And he dances, and he yells;
Keeping time, time, time,
In a sort of Runic rhyme,
    To the paean of the bells—
    Of the bells:
Keeping time, time, time,
In a sort of Runic rhyme,
    To the throbbing of the bells—

Of the bells, bells, bells—
    To the sobbing of the bells;
Keeping time, time, time,
    As he knells, knells, knells,
In a happy Runic rhyme,
    To the rolling of the bells—
Of the bells, bells, bells:
    To the tolling of the bells,
Of the bells, bells, bells, bells—
    Bells, bells, bells—
To the moaning and the groaning of the bells.

ANNABEL LEE

It was many and many a year ago,
    In a kingdom by the sea,
That a maiden there lived whom you may know
    By the name of Annabel Lee;
And this maiden she lived with no other thought
    Than to love and be loved by me.

I was a child and she was a child,
    In this kingdom by the sea;
But we loved with a love which was more than love—
    I and my Annabel Lee;
With a love that the wingèd seraphs of Heaven
    Coveted her and me.

And this was the reason that, long ago,
    In this kingdom by the sea,
A wind blew out of a cloud by night
    Chilling my Annabel Lee;
So that her highborn kinsmen came
    And bore her away from me,
To shut her up in a sepulcher
    In this kingdom by the sea.

The angels, not half so happy in Heaven,
    Went envying her and me—
Yes! that was the reason (as all men know,
    In this kingdom by the sea)
That the wind came out of the cloud by night,
    Chilling and killing my Annabel Lee.

But our love it was stronger by far than the love
    Of those who were older than we—
    Of many far wiser than we—
And neither the angels in Heaven above,
    Nor the demons down under the sea,
Can ever dissever my soul from the soul
    Of the beautiful Annabel Lee.

For the moon never beams without bringing me dreams
    Of the beautiful Annabel Lee;
And the stars never rise but I feel the bright eyes
    Of the beautiful Annabel Lee;
And so, all the nighttide, I lie down by the side
Of my darling, my darling, my life and my bride,
    In her sepulcher there by the sea,
    In her tomb by the sounding sea.

SONNET—SILENCE

There are some qualities—some incorporate things,
 That have a double life, which thus is made
A type of that twin entity which springs
 From matter and light, evinced in solid and shade.
There is a twofold *Silence*—sea and shore—
 Body and soul. One dwells in lonely places,
 Newly with grass o'ergrown; some solemn graces,
Some human memories and tearful lore,
Render him terrorless: his name's "No More."
He is the corporate Silence: dread him not!
 No power hath he of evil in himself;
But should some urgent fate (untimely lot!)
 Bring thee to meet his shadow (nameless elf,
That haunteth the lone regions where hath trod
No foot of man), commend thyself to God!

To One in Paradise

Thou wast all that to me, love,
   For which my soul did pine—
A green isle in the sea, love,
   A fountain and a shrine,
All wreathed with fairy fruits and flowers,
   And all the flowers were mine.

Ah, dream too bright to last!
   Ah, starry Hope! that didst arise
But to be overcast!
   A voice from out the Future cries,
"On! on!"—but o'er the Past
   (Dim gulf!) my spirit hovering lies
Mute, motionless, aghast!

For, alas! alas! with me
   The light of Life is o'er!
"No more—no more—no more—"

To One in Paradise

(Such language holds the solemn sea
　　To the sands upon the shore)
Shall bloom the thunder-blasted tree
　　Or the stricken eagle soar!

And all my days are trances,
　　And all my nightly dreams
Are where thy gray eye glances,
　　And where thy footstep gleams—
In what ethereal dances,
　　By what eternal streams.

THE RAVEN

Once upon a midnight dreary, while I pondered, weak
and weary,
Over many a quaint and curious volume of forgotten
lore,
While I nodded, nearly napping, suddenly there came
a tapping,
As of someone gently rapping, rapping at my chamber
door.
" 'Tis some visitor," I muttered, "tapping at my chamber
door—
Only this, and nothing more."

Ah, distinctly I remember it was in the bleak December,
And each separate dying ember wrought its ghost upon
      the floor.
Eagerly I wished the morrow;—vainly I had sought to
      borrow
From my books surcease of sorrow—sorrow for the lost
      Lenore—
For the rare and radiant maiden whom the angels name
      Lenore—
          Nameless here forevermore.

And the silken sad uncertain rustling of each purple
      curtain
Thrilled me—filled me with fantastic terrors never felt
      before;
So that now, to still the beating of my heart, I
      stood repeating,
" 'Tis some visitor entreating entrance at my chamber
      door—
Some late visitor entreating entrance at my chamber
      door;—
          This it is, and nothing more."

Presently my soul grew stronger; hesitating then no
    longer,
"Sir," said I, "or Madam, truly your forgiveness I
    implore;
But the fact is I was napping, and so gently you came
    rapping,
And so faintly you came tapping, tapping at my chamber
    door,
That I scarce was sure I heard you,"—here I opened
    wide the door;—
        Darkness there, and nothing more.

Deep into that darkness peering, long I stood there
    wondering, fearing,
Doubting, dreaming dreams no mortals ever dared to
    dream before;
But the silence was unbroken, and the stillness gave no
    token,
And the only word there spoken was the whispered
    word, "Lenore!"
This I whispered, and an echo murmured back the
    word, "Lenore!"—
        Merely this, and nothing more.

Back into the chamber turning, all my soul within me
    burning,
Soon again I heard a tapping somewhat louder than
    before.
"Surely," said I, "surely that is something at my window
    lattice:
Let me see, then, what thereat is, and this mystery
    explore—
Let my heart be still a moment and this mystery
    explore;—
        'Tis the wind and nothing more."

Open here I flung the shutter, when, with many a flirt
    and flutter,
In there stepped a stately raven of the saintly days of
    yore;
Not the least obeisance made he; not a minute stopped
    or stayed he;
But, with mien of lord or lady, perched above my
    chamber door—
Perched upon a bust of Pallas just above my chamber
    door—
        Perched, and sat, and nothing more.

Then this ebony bird beguiling my sad fancy into
    smiling,
By the grave and stern decorum of the countenance it
    wore,
"Though thy crest be shorn and shaven, thou," I said,
    "art sure no craven,
Ghastly grim and ancient raven wandering from the
    Nightly shore—
Tell me what thy lordly name is on the Night's
    Plutonian shore!"
        Quoth the Raven, "Nevermore."

Much I marveled this ungainly fowl to hear discourse
    so plainly,
Though its answer little meaning—little relevancy bore;
For we cannot help agreeing that no living human
    being
Ever yet was blest with seeing bird above his chamber
    door—
Bird or beast upon the sculptured bust above his chamber
    door,
        With such name as "Nevermore."

But the raven, sitting lonely on the placid bust, spoke
    only
That one word, as if his soul in that one word he did
    outpour.
Nothing further then he uttered—not a feather then he
    fluttered—
Till I scarcely more than muttered, "other friends have
    flown before—
On the morrow *he* will leave me, as my hopes have
    flown before."
        Then the bird said, "Nevermore."

Startled at the stillness broken by reply so aptly spoken,
"Doubtless," said I, "what it utters is its only stock and
    store,
Caught from some unhappy master whom unmerciful
    Disaster
Followed fast and followed faster till his songs one
    burden bore—
Till the dirges of his Hope that melancholy burden
    bore
        Of 'Never—nevermore.' "

THE RAVEN

But the Raven still beguiling all my fancy into
   smiling,
Straight I wheeled a cushioned seat in front of bird,
   and bust and door;
Then upon the velvet sinking, I betook myself to
   linking
Fancy unto fancy, thinking what this ominous bird of
   yore—
What this grim, ungainly, ghastly, gaunt, and ominous
   bird of yore
      Meant in croaking "Nevermore."

This I sat engaged in guessing, but no syllable
   expressing
To the fowl whose fiery eyes now burned into my
   bosom's core;
This and more I sat divining, with my head at ease
   reclining
On the cushion's velvet lining that the lamplight gloated
   o'er,
But whose velvet-violet lining with the lamplight
   gloating o'er,
      She shall press, ah, nevermore!

Then methought the air grew denser, perfumed from
    an unseen censer
Swung by seraphim whose footfalls tinkled on the tufted
    floor.
"Wretch," I cried, "thy God hath lent thee—by these
    angels he hath sent thee
Respite—respite and nepenthe, from thy memories of
    Lenore!
Quaff, oh quaff this kind nepenthe and forget this lost
    Lenore!"
        Quoth the Raven, "Nevermore."

"Prophet!" said I, "thing of evil!—prophet still, if
    bird or devil!—
Whether Tempter sent, or whether tempest tossed thee
    here ashore,
Desolate yet all undaunted, on this desert land
    enchanted—
On this home by horror haunted—tell me truly, I
    implore—
Is there—is there balm in Gilead?—tell me—tell me,
    I implore!"
        Quoth the Raven, "Nevermore."

"Prophet!" said I, "thing of evil—prophet still, if bird
    or devil!
By that Heaven that bends above us—by that God we
    both adore—
Tell this soul with sorrow laden if, within the distant
    Aidenn,
It shall clasp a sainted maiden whom the angels name
    Lenore—
Clasp a rare and radiant maiden whom the angels name
    Lenore."
        Quoth the Raven, "Nevermore."

"Be that word our sign in parting, bird or fiend," I
    shrieked, upstarting—
"Get thee back into the tempest and the Night's
    Plutonian shore!
Leave no black plume as a token of that lie thy soul
    hath spoken!
Leave my loneliness unbroken!—quit the bust above my
    door!
Take thy beak from out my heart, and take thy form
    from off my door!"
        Quoth the Raven, "Nevermore."

And the Raven, never flitting, still is sitting, still is
    sitting
On the pallid bust of Pallas just above my chamber
    door;
And his eyes have all the seeming of a demon's that is
    dreaming,
And the lamplight o'er him streaming throws his shadow
    on the floor;
And my soul from out that shadow that lies floating on
    the floor
        Shall be lifted—nevermore!

LENORE

Ah, broken is the golden bowl! the spirit flown forever!

Let the bell toll!—a saintly soul floats on the Stygian
river;

And, Guy de Vere, hast thou no tear?—weep now or
nevermore!

See! on yon drear and rigid bier low lies thy love,
Lenore!

Come! let the burial rite be read—the funeral song be
sung!—

An anthem for the queenliest dead that ever died so
young—

A dirge for her the doubly dead in that she died so
young.

"Wretches! ye loved her for her wealth and hated her
     for her pride,
And when she fell in feeble health, ye blessed her—
     that she died!
How shall the ritual, then, be read?—the requiem how
     be sung
By you—by yours, the evil eye,—by yours, the
     slanderous tongue
That did to death the innocence that died, and died so
     young?"

Peccavimus; but rave not thus! and let a Sabbath song
Go up to God so solemnly the dead may feel no wrong
The sweet Lenore hath "gone before," with Hope, that
     flew beside,
Leaving thee wild for the dear child that should have
     been thy bride—
For her, the fair and *debonair*, that now so lowly lies,
The life upon her yellow hair but not within her eyes—
The life still there, upon her hair—the death upon her
     eyes.

"Avaunt! avaunt! from fiends below, the indignant
     ghost is riven—
From Hell unto a high estate far up within the
     Heaven—
From grief and groan, to a golden throne, beside the
     King of Heaven!
Let no bell toll, then,—lest her soul, amid its hallowed
     mirth,
Should catch the note as it doth float up from the
     damnèd Earth!
And I!—tonight my heart is light:—no dirge will I
     upraise,
But waft the angel on her flight with a Paean of old
     days!"

DREAMS

Oh! that my young life were a lasting dream!
My spirit not awakening, till the beam
Of an Eternity should bring the morrow.
Yes! tho' that long dream were of hopeless sorrow,
'Twere better than the cold reality
Of waking life, to him whose heart must be,
And hath been still, upon the lovely earth,
A chaos of deep passion, from his birth.
But should it be—that dream eternally
Continuing—as dreams have been to me
In my young boyhood—should it thus be given,
'Twere folly still to hope for higher Heaven.
For I have revell'd, when the sun was bright
I' the summer sky, in dreams of living light
And loveliness,—have left my very heart
In climes of my imagining, apart.
From mine own home, with beings that have been
Of mine own thought—what more could I have seen?

'Twas once—and only once—and the wild hour
From my remembrance shall not pass—some power
Or spell had bound me—'twas the chilly wind
Came o'er me in the night, and left behind
Its image on my spirit—or the moon
Shone on my slumbers in her lofty noon
Too coldly—or the stars—howe'er it was
That dream was as that night-wind—let it pass.
I *have been* happy, tho' in a dream.
I have been happy—and I love the theme:
Dreams! in their vivid coloring of life,
As in that fleeting, shadowy, misty strife
Of semblance with reality, which brings
To the delirious eye, more lovely things
Of Paradise and Love—and all our own!
Than young Hope in his sunniest hour hath known.

To Helen

I saw thee once—once only—years ago:
I must not say how many—but not many.
It was a July midnight; and from out
A full-orbed moon, that, like thine own soul, soaring,
Sought a precipitate pathway up through heaven,
There fell a silvery-silken veil of light,
With quietude, and sultriness, and slumber,
Upon the upturned faces of a thousand
Roses that grew in an enchanted garden,
Where no wind dared to stir, unless on tiptoe—
Fell on the upturn'd faces of these roses
That gave out, in return for the love-light,
Their odorous souls in an ecstatic death—
Fell on the upturn'd faces of these roses
That smiled and died in this parterre, enchanted
By thee, and by the poetry of thy presence.
Clad all in white, upon a violet bank
I saw thee half-reclining; while the moon
Fell on the upturn'd faces of the roses,
And on thine own, upturn'd—alas, in sorrow!

Was it not Fate, that, on this July midnight—
Was it not Fate, (whose name is also Sorrow,)
That bade me pause before that garden gate,
To breathe the incense of those slumbering roses?

TO HELEN

No footstep stirred: the hated world all slept,
Save only thee and me. (Oh, Heaven!—oh, God!
How my heart beats in coupling those two words!)
Save only thee and me. I paused—I looked—
And in an instant all things disappeared.
(Ah, bear in mind this garden was enchanted!)

The pearly luster of the moon went out:
The mossy banks and the meandering paths,
The happy flowers and the repining trees,
Were seen no more: the very roses' odors
Died in the arms of the adoring airs.
All—all expired save thee—save less than thou:
Save only the divine light in thine eyes—
Save but the soul in thine uplifted eyes.

To Helen

I saw but them—they were the world to me!
I saw but them—saw only them for hours,
Saw only them until the moon went down.
What wild heart-histories seemed to lie enwritten
Upon those crystalline, celestial spheres!
How dark a woe, yet how sublime a hope!
How silently serene a sea of pride!
How daring an ambition; yet how deep—
How fathomless a capacity for love!

But now, at length, dear Dian sank from sight,
Into a western couch of thundercloud;
And thou, a ghost, amid the entombing trees
Didst glide away. *Only thine eyes remained;*
They *would not go*—they never yet have gone.
Lighting my lonely pathway home that night,
They have not left me (as my hopes have) since;
They follow me—they lead me through the years.

To Helen

They are my ministers—yet I their slave.
Their office is to illumine and enkindle—
My duty, *to be saved* by their bright light,
And purified in their electric fire,
And sanctified in their elysian fire.
They fill my soul with Beauty (which is Hope),
And are far up in Heaven—the stars I kneel to
In the sad, silent watches of my night;
While even in the meridian glare of day
I see them still—two sweetly scintillant
Venuses, unextinguished by the sun!

The Haunted Palace

In the greenest of our valleys
    By good angels tenanted,
Once a fair and stately palace—
    Radiant palace—reared its head.
In the monarch Thought's dominion—
    It stood there!
Never seraph spread a pinion
    Over fabric half so fair!

Banners yellow, glorious, golden,
    On its roof did float and flow,
(This—all this—was in the olden
    Time long ago,)
And every gentle air that dallied,
    In that sweet day,
Along the ramparts plumed and pallid,
    A wingèd odor went away.

THE HAUNTED PALACE

Wanderers in that happy valley,
　　Through two luminous windows, saw
Spirits moving musically,
　　To a lute's well-tunèd law,
Round about a throne where, sitting
　　(Porphyrogene!)
In state his glory well befitting,
　　The ruler of the realm was seen.

And all with pearl and ruby glowing
　　Was the fair palace door,
Through which came flowing, flowing, flowing,
　　And sparkling evermore,
A troop of Echoes, whose sweet duty
　　Was but to sing,
In voices of surpassing beauty,
　　The wit and wisdom of their king.

But evil things, in robes of sorrow,
    Assailed the monarch's high estate.
(Ah, let us mourn!—for never morrow
    Shall dawn upon him desolate!)
And round about his home the glory
    That blushed and bloomed,
Is but a dim-remembered story
    Of the old time entombed.

And travelers, now, within that valley,
    Through the red-litten windows see
Vast forms, that move fantastically
    To a discordant melody,
While, like a ghastly rapid river,
    Through the pale door
A hideous throng rush out forever
    And laugh—but smile no more.

A Dream Within a Dream

Take this kiss upon the brow!
And, in parting from you now,
Thus much let me avow—
You are not wrong, who deem
That my days have been a dream;
Yet if hope has flown away
In a night, or in a day,
In a vision, or in none,
Is it therefore the less *gone?*
All that we see or seem
Is but a dream within a dream.

I stand amid the roar
Of a surf-tormented shore,
And I hold within my hand
Grains of the golden sand—
How few! yet how they creep
Through my fingers to the deep,
While I weep—while I weep!
O God! can I not grasp
Them with a tighter clasp?
O God! can I not save
One from the pitiless wave?
Is *all* that we see or seem
But a dream within a dream?

THE CITY IN THE SEA

Lo! Death has reared himself a throne
In a strange city lying alone
Far down within the dim West,
Where the good and the bad and the worst and the best
Have gone to their eternal rest.
There shrines and palaces and towers
(Time-eaten towers that tremble not!)
Resemble nothing that is ours.
Around, by lifting winds forgot,
Resignedly beneath the sky
The melancholy waters lie.

The City in the Sea

No rays from the holy heaven come down
On the long nighttime of that town;
But light from out the lurid sea
Streams up the turrets silently—
Gleams up the pinnacles far and free—
Up domes—up spires—up kingly halls—
Up fanes—up Babylon-like walls—
Up shadowy long-forgotten bowers
Of sculptured ivy and stone flowers—
Up many and many a marvelous shrine
Whose wreathèd friezes intertwine
The viol, the violet, and the vine.

Resignedly beneath the sky
The melancholy waters lie.
So blend the turrets and shadows there
That all seem pendulous in air,
While from a proud tower in the town
Death looks gigantically down.

There open fanes and gaping graves
Yawn level with the luminous waves;
But not the riches there that lie
In each idol's diamond eye—
Not the gaily jeweled dead
Tempt the waters from their bed;
For no ripples curl, alas!
Along that wilderness of glass—
No swellings tell that winds may be
Upon some far-off happier sea—
No heavings hint that winds have been
On seas less hideously serene.

But lo, a stir is in the air!
The wave—there is a movement there!
As if the towers had thrust aside,
In slightly sinking, the dull tide—
As if their tops had feebly given
A void within the filmy Heaven.
The waves have now a redder glow—
The hours are breathing faint and low—
And when, amid no earthly moans,
Down, down that town shall settle hence,
Hell, rising from a thousand thrones,
Shall do it reverence.

To F——

Beloved! amid the earnest woes
    That crowd around my earthly path—
(Drear path, alas! where grows
Not even one lonely rose)—
    My soul at least a solace hath
In dreams of thee, and therein knows
An Eden of bland repose.

And thus thy memory is to me
    Like some enchanted far-off isle
In some tumultuous sea—
Some ocean throbbing far and free
    With storms—but where meanwhile
Serenest skies continually
    Just o'er that one bright island smile.

ROMANCE

Romance, who loves to nod and sing,
With drowsy head and folded wing,
Among the green leaves as they shake
Far down within some shadowy lake,
To me a painted paroquet
Hath been—a most familiar bird—
Taught me my alphabet to say—
To lisp my very earliest word
While in the wild wood I did lie,
A child—with a most knowing eye.

Of late, eternal Condor years
So shake the very Heaven on high
With tumult as they thunder by,
I have no time for idle cares
Through gazing on the unquiet sky.
And when an hour with calmer wings
Its down upon my spirit flings—
That little time with lyre and rhyme
To while away—forbidden things!
My heart would feel to be a crime
Unless it trembled with the strings.

THE SLEEPER

At midnight, in the month of June,
I stand beneath the mystic moon.
An opiate vapor, dewy, dim,
Exhales from out her golden rim,
And, softly dripping, drop by drop,
Upon the quiet mountaintop,
Steals drowsily and musically
Into the universal valley.
The rosemary nods upon the grave;
The lily lolls upon the wave;
Wrapping the fog about its breast,
The ruin molders into rest;
Looking like Lethe, see! the lake
A conscious slumber seems to take,
And would not, for the world, awake.
All Beauty sleeps!—and lo! where lies
Irene, with her Destinies!

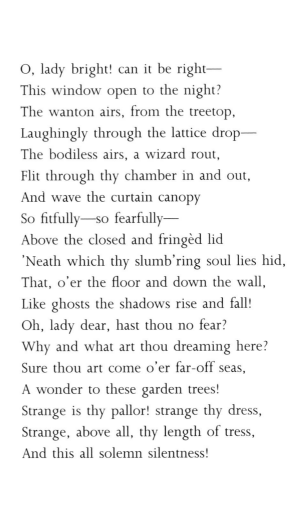

O, lady bright! can it be right—
This window open to the night?
The wanton airs, from the treetop,
Laughingly through the lattice drop—
The bodiless airs, a wizard rout,
Flit through thy chamber in and out,
And wave the curtain canopy
So fitfully—so fearfully—
Above the closed and fringèd lid
'Neath which thy slumb'ring soul lies hid,
That, o'er the floor and down the wall,
Like ghosts the shadows rise and fall!
Oh, lady dear, hast thou no fear?
Why and what art thou dreaming here?
Sure thou art come o'er far-off seas,
A wonder to these garden trees!
Strange is thy pallor! strange thy dress,
Strange, above all, thy length of tress,
And this all solemn silentness!

THE SLEEPER

The lady sleeps! Oh, may her sleep,
Which is enduring, so be deep!
Heaven have her in its sacred keep!
This chamber changed for one more holy,
This bed for one more melancholy,
I pray to God that she may lie
Forever with unopened eye,
While the pale sheeted ghosts go by!

My love, she sleeps! Oh, may her sleep
As it is lasting, so be deep!
Soft may the worms about her creep!
Far in the forest, dim and old,
For her may some tall vault unfold—
Some vault that oft has flung its black
And wingèd panels fluttering back,
Triumphant, o'er the crested palls,
Of her grand family funerals—
Some sepulcher, remote, alone,
Against whose portal she hath thrown,
In childhood, many an idle stone—
Some tomb from out whose sounding door
She ne'er shall force an echo more,
Thrilling to think, poor child of sin!
It was the dead who groaned within.

ULALUME

The skies they were ashen and sober;
    The leaves they were crisped and sere—
    The leaves they were withering and sere;
It was night in the lonesome October
    Of my most immemorial year;
It was hard by the dim lake of Auber,
    In the misty mid region of Weir—
It was down by the dank tarn of Auber,
    In the ghoul-haunted woodland of Weir.

Here once, through an alley Titanic,
    Of cypress, I roamed with my Soul—
    Of cypress, with Psyche, my Soul.

These were days when my heart was volcanic
    As the scoriac rivers that roll—
    As the lavas that restlessly roll
Their sulfurous currents down Yaanek
    In the ultimate climes of the pole—
That groan as they roll down Mount Yaanek
    In the realms of the boreal pole.

Our talk had been serious and sober,
    But our thoughts they were palsied and sere—
    Our memories were treacherous and sere—
For we knew not the month was October,
    And we marked not the night of the year—
    (Ah, night of all nights in the year!)
We noted not the dim lake of Auber—
    (Though once we had journeyed down here),
Remembered not the dank tarn of Auber,
    Nor the ghoul-haunted woodland of Weir.

And now, as the night was senescent,
    And star-dials pointed to morn—
    As the star-dials hinted of morn—
At the end of our path a liquescent
    And nebulous luster was born,
Out of which a miraculous crescent
    Arose with a duplicate horn—
Astarte's bediamonded crescent
    Distinct with its duplicate horn.

And I said—"She is warmer than Dian:
    She rolls through an ether of sighs—
    She revels in a region of sighs:
She has seen that the tears are not dry on
    These cheeks, where the worm never dies,
And has come past the stars of the Lion,
    To point us the path to the skies—
    To the Lethean peace of the skies—

Come up, in despite of the Lion,
    To shine on us with her bright eyes—
Come up through the lair of the Lion,
    With love in her luminous eyes."

But Psyche, uplifting her finger,
    Said—"Sadly this star I mistrust—
    Her pallor I strangely mistrust:—
Oh, hasten!—oh, let us not linger!
    Oh, fly!—let us fly!—for we must."
In terror she spoke, letting sink her
    Wings until they trailed in the dust—
In agony sobbed, letting sink her
    Plumes till they trailed in the dust—
    Till they sorrowfully trailed in the dust.

I replied—"This is nothing but dreaming:
    Let us on by this tremulous light!
    Let us bathe in this crystalline light!

Its Sybilic splendor is beaming
    With Hope and in Beauty tonight:
    See!—it flickers up the sky through the night!
Ah, we safely may trust to its gleaming,
    And be sure it will lead us aright—
We safely may trust to a gleaming
    That cannot but guide us aright,
    Since it flickers up to Heaven through the night."

Thus I pacified Psyche and kissed her,
    And tempted her out of her gloom—
    And conquered her scruples and gloom;
And we passed to the end of the vista,
    But were stopped by the door of a tomb—
    By the door of a legended tomb;
And I said—"What is written, sweet sister,
    On the door of this legended tomb?"

She replied—"Ulalume—Ulalume—
'Tis the vault of thy lost Ulalume!"

Then my heart it grew ashen and sober
    As the leaves that were crisped and sere—
    As the leaves that were withering and sere;
And I cried—"It was surely October
    On this very night of last year
    That I journeyed—I journeyed down here—
    That I brought a dread burden down here—
    On this night of all nights in the year,
    Ah, what demon has tempted me here?
Well I know, now, this dim lake of Auber—
    This misty mid region of Weir—
Well I know, now, this dank tarn of Auber,
    This ghoul-haunted woodland of Weir."

Eldorado

Gaily bedight,
A gallant knight,
In sunshine and in shadow,
Had journeyed long,
Singing a song,
In search of Eldorado.

But he grew old—
This knight so bold—
And o'er his heart a shadow
Fell as he found
No spot of ground
That looked like Eldorado.

And, as his strength
Failed him at length,
He met a pilgrim shadow—
"Shadow," said he,
"Where can it be—
This land of Eldorado?"

"Over the Mountains
Of the Moon,
Down the Valley of the Shadow,
Ride, boldly ride,"
The shade replied—
"If you seek for Eldorado!"

To the River ——

Fair river! in thy bright, clear flow
   Of crystal, wandering water,
Thou art an emblem of the glow
     Of beauty—the unhidden heart—
     The playful maziness of art
In old Alberto's daughter;

But when within thy wave she looks—
   Which glistens then, and trembles—
Why, then, the prettiest of brooks
   Her worshiper resembles;
For in my heart, as in thy stream,
   Her image deeply lies—
His heart which trembles at the beam
   Of her soul-searching eyes.

BRIDAL BALLAD

The ring is on my hand,
    And the wreath is on my brow;
Satin and jewels grand
Are all at my command,
    And I am happy now.

And my lord he loves me well;
    But, when first he breathed his vow,
I felt my bosom swell—
For the words rang as a knell,
And the voice seemed *his* who fell
In the battle down the dell,
    And who is happy now.

But he spoke to reassure me,
    And he kissed my pallid brow,
While a reverie came o'er me,
And to the churchyard bore me,
And I sighed to him before me,
Thinking him dead D'Elormie,
    "Oh, I am happy now!"

And thus the words were spoken,
   And this the plighted vow,
And, though my faith be broken,
And, though my heart be broken,
Here is a ring, as token
   That I am happy now!

Would God I could awaken!
   For I dream I know not how!
And my soul is sorely shaken
Lest an evil step be taken,
Lest the dead who is forsaken
   May not be happy now.

To my Mother

Because I feel that, in the heavens above,
    The angels, whispering to one another,
Can find, among their burning terms of love,
    None so devotional as that of "Mother,"
Therefore by that dear name I long have called you—
    You who are more than mother unto me,
And fill my heart of hearts, where Death installed you
    In setting my Virginia's spirit free.
My mother—my own mother, who died early,
    Was but the mother of myself; but you
Are mother to the one I loved so dearly,
    And thus are dearer than the mother I knew
By that infinity with which my wife
    Was dearer to my soul than its soul-life.

To Helen

Helen, thy beauty is to me
   Like those Nicean barks of yore,
That gently, o'er a perfumed sea,
   The weary, wayworn wanderer bore
   To his own native shore.

On desperate seas long wont to roam,
   Thy hyacinth hair, thy classic face,
Thy Naiad airs have brought me home
   To the glory that was Greece,
   And the grandeur that was Rome.

Lo! in yon brilliant window niche
   How statuelike I see thee stand,
The agate lamp within thy hand!
   Ah, Psyche, from the regions which
   Are Holy Land!

THE VALLEY OF UNREST

Once it smiled a silent dell
Where the people did not dwell;
They had gone unto the wars,
Trusting to the mild-eyed stars,
Nightly, from their azure towers,
To keep watch above the flowers,
In the midst of which all day
The red sunlight lazily lay.

THE VALLEY OF UNREST

Now each visitor shall confess
The sad valley's restlessness.
Nothing there is motionless—
Nothing save the airs that brood
Over the magic solitude.
Ah, by no wind are stirred those trees
That palpitate like the chill seas
Around the misty Hebrides!
Ah, by no wind those clouds are driven
That rustle through the unquiet Heaven
Uneasily, from morn till even,
Over the violets there that lie
In myriad types of the human eye—
Over the lilies there that wave
And weep above a nameless grave!
They wave:—from out their fragrant tops
Eternal dews come down in drops.
They weep:—from off their delicate stems
Perennial tears descend in gems.

To —— ——

Not long ago, the writer of these lines,
In the mad pride of intellectuality,
Maintained "the power of words"—denied that ever
A thought arose within the human brain
Beyond the utterance of the human tongue:
And now, as if in mockery of that boast,
Two words—two foreign soft dissyllables—
Italian tones, made only to be murmured
By angels dreaming in the moonlit "dew
That hangs like chains of pearl on Hermon hill,"
Have stirred from out the abysses of his heart,
Unthought-like thoughts that are the souls of thought,
Richer, far wilder, far diviner visions
Than even seraph harper, Israfel,
(Who has "the sweetest voice of all God's creatures,")
Could hope to utter. And I! my spells are broken.
The pen falls powerless from my shivering hand.
With thy dear name as text, though bidden by thee,
I cannot write—I cannot speak or think—
Alas, I cannot feel; for 'tis not feeling,
This standing motionless upon the golden
Threshold of the wide-open gate of dreams.
Gazing, entranced, adown the gorgeous vista,
And thrilling as I see, upon the right,
Upon the left, and all the way along,
Amid empurpled vapors, far away
To where the prospect terminates—*thee only*.

Israfel

And the angel Israfel, whose heartstrings are a lute, and who has the sweetest voice of all God's creatures.—Koran.

In Heaven a spirit doth dwell
   "Whose heartstrings are a lute;"
None sing so wildly well
As the angel Israfel,
And the giddy stars (so legends tell)
Ceasing their hymns, attend the spell
   Of his voice, all mute.

Tottering above
 In her highest noon,
 The enamored moon
Blushes with love,
 While, to listen, the red levin
 (With the rapid Pleiads, even,
 Which were seven,)
 Pauses in Heaven.

And they say (the starry choir
 And the other listening things)
That Israfeli's fire
Is owing to that lyre
 By which he sits and sings—
The trembling living wire
 Of those unusual strings.

But the skies that angel trod,
  Where deep thoughts are a duty—
Where Love's a grown-up God—
  Where the Houri glances are
Imbued with all the beauty
  Which we worship in a star.

Therefore thou art not wrong,
  Israfeli, who despisest
An unimpassioned song;
To thee the laurels belong,
  Best bard, because the wisest!
Merrily live, and long!

The ecstasies above
  With thy burning measures suit—
Thy grief, thy joy, thy hate, thy love,
  With the fervor of thy lute—
  Well may the stars be mute!

Yes, Heaven is thine; but this
   Is a world of sweets and sours;
   Our flowers are merely—flowers,
And the shadow of thy perfect bliss
   Is the sunshine of ours.

If I could dwell
Where Israfel
   Hath dwelt, and he where I,
He might not sing so wildly well
   A mortal melody,
While a bolder note than this might swell
   From my lyre within the sky.

SONG

I saw thee on thy bridal day—
  When a burning blush came o'er thee,
Though happiness around thee lay,
  The world all love before thee:

And in thine eye a kindling light
  (Whatever it might be)
Was all on Earth my aching sight
  Of Loveliness could see.

That blush, perhaps, was maiden shame—
  As such it well may pass—
Though its glow hath raised a fiercer flame
  In the breast of him, alas!

Who saw thee on that bridal day,
  When that deep blush would come o'er thee,
Though happiness around thee lay;
  The world all love before thee.

To ——

The bowers whereat, in dreams, I see
   The wantonest singing birds,
Are lips—and all thy melody
   Of lip-begotten words—

Thine eyes, in Heaven of heart enshrined,
   Then desolately fall,
O God! on my funereal mind
   Like starlight on a pall—

Thy heart—thy heart!—I wake and sigh,
   And sleep to dream till day
Of the truth that gold can never buy—
   Of the baubles that it may.

FAIRYLAND

Dim vales—and shadowy floods—
And cloudy-looking woods,
Whose forms we can't discover
For the tears that drip all over
Huge moons there wax and wane—
Again—again—again—
Every moment of the night—
Forever changing places—
And they put out the starlight
With the breath from their pale faces.
About twelve by the moon dial,
One more filmy than the rest
(A kind which, upon trial,
They have found to be the best)

Comes down—still down—and down,
With its center on the crown
Of a mountain's eminence,
While its wide circumference
In easy drapery falls
Over hamlets, over halls,
Wherever they may be—
O'er the strange woods—o'er the sea—
Over spirits on the wing—
Over every drowsy thing—
And buries them up quite
In a labyrinth of light—
And then, how deep!—O, deep!
Is the passion of their sleep.
In the morning they arise,
And their moony covering
Is soaring in the skies,
With the tempests as they toss,
Like——almost anything—
Or a yellow Albatross.

They use that moon no more
For the same end as before—
Videlicet a tent—
Which I think extravagant:
Its atomies, however,
Into a shower dissever,
Of which those butterflies,
Of Earth, who seek the skies,
And so come down again
(Never-contented things!)
Have brought a specimen
Upon their quivering wings.

A VALENTINE

[To translate the address, read the first letter of the first
line in connection with the second letter of the second
line, the third letter of the third line, the fourth of the
fourth, and so on to the end. The name will thus appear.]

For her this rhyme is penned, whose luminous eyes,
 Brightly expressive as the twins of Loeda,
Shall find her own sweet name, that, nestling lies
 Upon the page, enwrapped from every reader.
Search narrowly the lines!—they hold a treasure
 Divine—a talisman—an amulet
That must be worn *at heart*. Search well the measure—
 The words—the syllables! Do not forget
The trivialest point, or you may lose your labor!
 And yet there is in this no Gordian knot
Which one might not undo without a saber,
 If one could merely comprehend the plot.
Enwritten upon the leaf where now are peering
 Eyes scintillating soul, there lie *perdus*
Three eloquent words oft uttered in the hearing
 Of poets, by poets—as the name is a poet's too.
Its letters, although naturally lying
 Like the knight Pinto—Mendez Ferdinando—
Still form a synonym for Truth.—Cease trying!
 You will not read the riddle, though you do the best
  you *can* do.

DREAMLAND

By a route obscure and lonely,
Haunted by ill angels only,
Where an Eidolon, named NIGHT,
On a black throne reigns upright,
I have reached these lands but newly
From an ultimate dim Thule—
From a wild weird clime that lieth, sublime,
Out of SPACE—out of TIME.

Bottomless vales and boundless floods,
And chasms, and caves, and Titan woods,
With forms that no man can discover
For the tears that drip all over;

Mountains toppling evermore
Into seas without a shore;
Seas that restlessly aspire,
Surging, unto skies of fire;
Lakes that endlessly outspread
Their lone waters—lone and dead,—
Their still waters—still and chilly
With the snows of the lolling lily.

By the lakes that thus outspread
Their lone waters, lone and dead,—
Their sad waters, sad and chilly
With the snows of the lolling lily—
By the mountains—near the river
Murmuring lowly, murmuring ever,—
By the gray woods,—by the swamp
Where the toad and the newt encamp,—
By the dismal tarns and pools

DREAMLAND

Where dwell the Ghouls,—
By each spot the most unholy—
In each nook most melancholy,—
There the traveler meets aghast
Sheeted Memories of the Past—
Shrouded forms that start and sigh
As they pass the wanderer by—
White-robed forms of friends long given,
In agony, to the Earth—and Heaven.

For the heart whose woes are legion
'Tis a peaceful, soothing region—
For the spirit that walks in shadow
'Tis—oh, 'tis an Eldorado!
But the traveler, traveling through it,
May not—dare not openly view it!
Never its mysteries are exposed
To the weak human eye unclosed;

So wills its King, who hath forbid
The uplifting of the fringèd lid;
And thus the sad Soul that here passes
Beholds it but through darkened glasses.

By a route obscure and lonely,
Haunted by ill angels only,
Where an Eidolon, named Night,
On a black throne reigns upright,
I have wandered home but newly
From this ultimate dim Thule.

ALONE

From childhood's hour I have not been
As others were; I have not seen
As others saw; I could not bring
My passions from a common spring.
From the same source I have not taken
My sorrow; I could not awaken
My heart to joy at the same tone;
And all I loved I loved alone.
Then—in my childhood, in the dawn
Of a most stormy life—was drawn
From every depth of good and ill
The mystery which binds me still:

From the torrent, or the fountain,
From the red cliff of the mountain,
From the sun that round me rolled
In its autumn tint of gold,
From the lightning in the sky
As it passed me flying by,
From the thunder and the storm,
And the cloud that took the form
(When the rest of Heaven was blue)
Of a demon in my view.

TAMERLANE

Kind solace in a dying hour!
   Such, father, is not (now) my theme—
I will not madly deem that power
     Of Earth may shrive me of the sin
     Unearthly pride hath revell'd in—
I have no time to dote or dream:
You call it hope—that fire of fire!
It is but agony of desire:
If I *can* hope—O God! I can—
   Its fount is holier—more divine—
I would not call thee fool, old man,
   But such is not a gift of thine.

Know thou the secret of a spirit
   Bow'd from its wild pride into shame.
O yearning heart! I did inherit
   Thy withering portion with the fame,
The searing glory which hath shone
Amid the jewels of my throne,
Halo of Hell! and with a pain
Not Hell shall make me fear again—
O craving heart, for the lost flowers
And sunshine of my summer hours!
The undying voice of that dead time,
With its interminable chime,
Rings, in the spirit of a spell,
Upon thy emptiness—a knell.

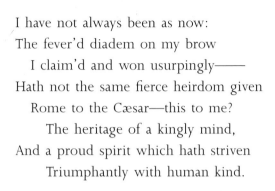

I have not always been as now:
The fever'd diadem on my brow
   I claim'd and won usurpingly——
Hath not the same fierce heirdom given
   Rome to the Cæsar—this to me?
      The heritage of a kingly mind,
And a proud spirit which hath striven
      Triumphantly with human kind.

On mountain soil I first drew life:
   The mists of the Taglay have shed
   Nightly their dews upon my head,
And, I believe, the wingèd strife
And tumult of the headlong air
Have nestled in my very hair.

So late from Heaven—that dew—it fell
　　('Mid dreams of an unholy night)
Upon me with the touch of Hell,
　　While the red flashing of the light
From clouds that hung, like banners, o'er,
　　Appeared to my half-closing eye
　　The pageantry of monarchy,
And the deep trumpet-thunder's roar
　　Came hurriedly upon me, telling
　　　Of human battle, where my voice,
My own voice, silly child!—was swelling
　　　(O! how my spirit would rejoice,
And leap within me at the cry)
The battlecry of Victory!

The rain came down upon my head
   Unshelter'd—and the heavy wind
   Rendered me mad and deaf and blind.
It was but man, I thought, who shed
   Laurels upon me: and the rush—
The torrent of the chilly air
   Gurgled within my ear the crush
Of empires—with the captive's prayer—
The hum of suitors—and the tone
Of flattery 'round a sovereign's throne.

My passions, from that hapless hour,
   Usurp'd a tyranny which men
Have deem'd since I have reach'd to power,
    My innate nature—be it so:
   But father, there liv'd one who, then,
Then—in my boyhood—when their fire
   Burn'd with a still intenser glow,
(For passion must, with youth, expire)
   E'en *then* who knew this iron heart
   In woman's weakness had a part.

I have no words—alas!—to tell
The loveliness of loving well!
Nor would I now attempt to trace
The more than beauty of a face
Whose lineaments, upon my mind,
Are——shadows on th' unstable wind:
Thus I remember having dwelt
  Some page of early lore upon,
With loitering eye, till I have felt
The letters—with their meaning—melt
  To fantasies—with none.

O, she was worthy of all love!
  Love—as in infancy was mine—
'Twas such as angel minds above
  Might envy; her young heart the shrine
On which my every hope and thought
  Were incense—then a goodly gift,
    For they were childish and upright—
Pure—as her young example taught:
  Why did I leave it, and, adrift,
    Trust to the fire within, for light?

We grew in age—and love—together,
   Roaming the forest, and the wild;
My breast her shield in wintry weather—
   And, when the friendly sunshine smil'd
And she would mark the opening skies,
I saw no Heaven—but in her eyes.

Young Love's first lesson is—the heart:
   For 'mid that sunshine, and those smiles,
When, from our little cares apart,
   And laughing at her girlish wiles,
I'd throw me on her throbbing breast,
   And pour my spirit out in tears—
There was no need to speak the rest—
   No need to quiet any fears
Of her—who ask'd no reason why,
But turned on me her quiet eye!

Yet more than worthy of the love
My spirit struggled with, and strove,
When, on the mountain peak, alone,
Ambition lent it a new tone—
I had no being—but in thee:
   The world, and all it did contain
In the earth—the air—the sea—
   Its joy—its little lot of pain
That was new pleasure—the ideal,
   Dim vanities of dreams by night—
And dimmer nothings which were real—
   (Shadows—and a more shadowy light!)
Parted upon their misty wings,
   And, so, confusedly, became
   Thine image, and—a name—a name!
Two separate—yet most intimate things.

I was ambitious—have you known
   The passion, father? You have not:
A cottager, I mark'd a throne
Of half the world as all my own,
   And murmur'd at such lowly lot—
But, just like any other dream,
   Upon the vapor of the dew
My own had past, did not the beam
   Of beauty which did while it thro'
The minute—the hour—the day—oppress
My mind with double loveliness.

We walk'd together on the crown
Of a high mountain which look'd down
Afar from its proud natural towers
   Of rock and forest, on the hills—
The dwindled hills! begirt with bowers,
   And shouting with a thousand rills.

I spoke to her of power and pride,
    But mystically—in such guise
That she might deem it naught beside
    The moment's converse; in her eyes
I read, perhaps too carelessly—
    A mingled feeling with my own—
The flush on her bright cheek, to me
    Seem'd to become a queenly throne
Too well that I should let it be
    Light in the wilderness alone.

I wrapp'd myself in grandeur then,
  And donn'd a visionary crown—
    Yet it was not that Fantasy
    Had thrown her mantle over me—
But that, among the rabble—men,
  Lion ambition is chained down—
And crouches to a keeper's hand—
Not so in deserts where the grand—
The wild—the terrible conspire
With their own breath to fan his fire.

Look 'round thee now on Samarcand!
  Is not she queen of Earth? her pride
Above all cities? in her hand
  Their destinies? in all beside
Of glory which the world hath known
Stands she not nobly and alone?
Falling—her veriest steppingstone
Shall form the pedestal of a throne—

And who her sovereign? Timour—he
  Whom the astonished people saw
Striding o'er empires haughtily
  A diadem'd outlaw!

O, human love! thou spirit given,
On Earth, of all we hope in Heaven!
Which fall'st into the soul like rain
Upon the Siroc-wither'd plain,
And, failing in thy power to bless,
But leav'st the heart a wilderness!
Idea! which bindest life around
With music of so strange a sound,
And beauty of so wild a birth—
Farewell! for I have won the Earth.

When Hope, the eagle that tower'd, could see
  No cliff beyond him in the sky,

His pinions were bent droopingly—
    And homeward turn'd his soften'd eye.
'Twas sunset: when the sun will part
There comes a sullenness of heart
To him who still would look upon
The glory of the summer sun.
That soul will hate the ev'ning mist,
So often lovely, and will list
To the sound of the coming darkness (known
To those whose spirits hearken) as one
Who, in a dream of night, would fly
But cannot, from a danger nigh.

What tho' the moon—the white moon
Shed all the splendor of her noon,
Her smile is chilly, and her beam,
In that time of dreariness, will seem

(So like you gather in your breath)
A portrait taken after death.
And boyhood is a summer sun
Whose waning is the dreariest one—
For all we live to know is known,
And all we seek to keep hath flown—
Let life, then, as the dayflower, fall
With the noonday beauty—which is all.

I reach'd my home—my home no more—
   For all had flown who made it so.
I pass'd from out its mossy door,
   And, tho' my tread was soft and low,
A voice came from the threshold stone
Of one whom I had earlier known—
O, I defy thee, Hell, to show
On beds of fire that burn below,
A humbler heart—a deeper woe.

Father, I firmly do believe—
   I know—for Death, who comes for me
      From regions of the blest afar,
Where there is nothing to deceive,
     Hath left his iron gate ajar,
   And rays of truth you cannot see
   Are flashing thro' Eternity——
I do believe that Eblis hath
A snare in every human path—
Else how, when in the holy grove
I wandered of the idol, Love,
Who daily scents his snowy wings
With incense of burnt offerings
From the most unpolluted things,
Whose pleasant bowers are yet so riven
Above with trellis'd rays from Heaven
No mote may shun—no tiniest fly—
The light'ning of his eagle eye—
How was it that Ambition crept,
   Unseen, amid the revels there,
Till growing bold, he laughed and leapt
   In the tangles of Love's very hair?